A SEAT AT THE TABLE

THE NANCY PELOSI STORY

Elisa Boxer

illustrated by
Laura Freeman

Crown Books for Young Readers ♛ New York

The mayor's daughter watched out the window as families lined up at the door, looking for help.

Baltimore's first Italian American mayor saw himself in these strangers.
Once a week, he would welcome them in, give them a seat at the table.

Those who were struggling suddenly felt seen.

But it was the mayor's wife who made them finally feel heard.

When the mayor went off to city hall, she stayed home and listened to their stories.

Little Nancy listened too.

She heard her mother speak Italian to immigrants who couldn't understand English.

Some were sick. Her mother helped them get beds at City Hospital.

Some were out of work and homeless. Her mother helped them find jobs and places to live.

Some were hungry. Her mother added more stew to the pot on the stove.

"My father did the day job of mayor," Nancy recalled, "but my mother was his unpaid partner in public service. She showed people their value."

When it was time for them to leave, Nancy noticed they held their heads a little higher.

For years, Nancy watched her father work hard as mayor.
And she watched her mother work just as hard—
helping their community.
And helping her husband get reelected.

Behind the scenes, the mayor's
wife hustled . . .
organizing meetings,

stuffing envelopes,

making phone calls,

and ringing doorbells,

so that her husband could keep getting
the votes that would keep him in office.

Women, after all, were supposed to stay out of the spotlight, supporting men in positions of power.

In high school, Nancy had an "encounter with history," when her father brought her along to a special dinner. The guest of honor? A rising political star by the name of John F. Kennedy.

She got to sit next to him at the head table.

In college, she sat on the Capitol steps as he was sworn in as President Kennedy. She was inspired by "his electrifying call to public service" and carried that inspiration with her through the years as she grew up, got married, and moved across the country to San Francisco.

While raising five children, she hustled behind the scenes, just like her mother had done . . . organizing meetings,

stuffing envelopes,

making phone calls,

and ringing doorbells, to help candidates win elections.

Until one day, she was asked to *be* a candidate.

Her dear friend Sala Burton was a congresswoman in the U.S. House of Representatives.

She was also very sick, so there was going to be a special election to find her replacement. She called Nancy to her bedside.

Me? Run for office? Nancy couldn't believe what her friend was asking.

But Sala knew how hard Nancy would work to help immigrants and other families facing challenges. She wouldn't take no for an answer.

"Sometimes it takes the encouragement of someone who knows us well to propel us forward in ways we never would have dreamed," Nancy said, looking back.

Her opponents made fun of her for being a housewife. They said she didn't stand a chance of being a congresswoman.

Nancy didn't listen.

She was too busy raising one million dollars, gathering four thousand volunteers,

organizing meetings to get *herself* elected,

stuffing envelopes with her picture inside,

making phone calls, ringing doorbells,

and showing up at bus stops to introduce herself:

"I'm Nancy Pelosi, and I'm running for Congress."

Her campaign slogan was

"A VOICE THAT WILL BE HEARD."

Her opponents thought that was nonsense, since no one even knew who she was.

But they were about to. . . .

In 1987, Nancy Pelosi was sworn in as a U.S. congresswoman.

She asked how much time was allowed for her speech. She was told that new lawmakers didn't get to make speeches.

But Nancy hadn't come this far to keep quiet.

She gave voice to everything she'd be fighting for in Congress:

More money for schools . . .

More money for sick people and struggling families . . .

Laws promoting peace . . .

Laws protecting the environment . . .

Laws providing equal treatment for everyone, no matter their gender . . .

or where they're from . . .

or who they love.

"What is in your heart is what you will have the courage to fight for," she later said.

Year after year, she kept fighting, kept getting reelected, and kept climbing the ranks, right up to minority leader—the head of the Democrats when there are more Republicans in the House of Representatives.

Nancy was the first woman ever to lead a political party in Congress.

As she sat down with President George W. Bush in her first official meeting as Democratic leader, she thought of all the fearless females who had fought so hard for women's rights.

She could feel them with her.

She could hear them say, *"At last, we have a seat at the table."*

But Nancy wanted a seat "at the *head* of the table."

In 2007, twenty years after she first came to Congress, Nancy Pelosi was elected Speaker of the House of Representatives—the leader of the Democrats when they are in the majority.

This made her second in line for the presidency and the highest-ranking female in the history of the federal government.

People sometimes use the phrase "glass ceiling" to describe barriers blocking women from upper-level jobs typically held by men.

The U.S. Capitol is made of marble.

"For our daughters and granddaughters," Speaker Pelosi said on the day she was sworn in, "today we have broken the marble ceiling."

Three days later, the highest-ranking woman in American political history went back to where it all began—her childhood home in Baltimore, where she would watch out the window as strangers lined up on the street to ask for her father's help.

That street was renamed Via Nancy D'Alesandro Pelosi in her honor.

"I wanted to come back here and say thank you," she told the crowd gathered in celebration. "Every step that I took to the speakership began in this neighborhood."

Earlier that day, she'd placed a bouquet of white roses at a statue of her father—the man who'd welcomed anyone who needed help to take a seat at the table . . . and inspired his daughter to take hers.

She stayed Speaker of the House for four years, until
Republicans outnumbered Democrats after another election.

With her political party no longer in control, many people
expected Nancy to step down as leader.

Instead, she stepped up her efforts.

Nancy crisscrossed the country, raising money and hopes for a
future that included more women in politics.

"When women succeed, America succeeds," she said. "They're going to win, and they're going to make a tremendous difference."

She was right.

In 2018, a record-breaking number of women won seats in the nation's capital, including the first Muslim women, the first Native American women, and the youngest woman ever elected to Congress.

And a seventy-eight-year-old grandmother made history for the second time, reclaiming her role as House Speaker.

Nancy's triumphant return marked a momentous year for women's rights.

"I am particularly proud to be the woman Speaker of the House of this Congress," she said, "which marks one hundred years of women winning the right to vote."

Her husband cheered her on from the gallery.

Dozens of children, including her nine grandchildren, filled the House floor. She called them all up to stand with her.

Two years later, this House was stormed by rioters trying to stop a crucial vote to confirm newly elected President Joe Biden. The mob ransacked Nancy Pelosi's office, stole her laptop, and shattered her mirror. But not her courage.

She had just been elected to her fourth term as Speaker. In what she later called "a message of strength," she brought lawmakers back into session to finish the vote.

And then, in a voice that will continue to be heard throughout history, Speaker Pelosi took to the podium and took back America's House.

AUTHOR'S NOTE

When Nancy Pelosi first arrived in the nation's capital, there were 510 men and only 25 women in Congress. The cigar smoke that often accompanied "old-boy politics" wafted through the chamber. One of her first moves as House Speaker was to ban smoking in the Capitol. She wanted to change the old guard and clear the air. She also wanted to send a message to women and girls that "anything is possible for them, that women can achieve power, wield power, and breathe the air at that altitude." She harnessed that power herself in so many historic ways, including being the only House Speaker ever to bring forward two articles of impeachment against a president.

But for Speaker Pelosi, power is nothing without purpose. She has consistently used her position to fight for women's rights, including affordable childcare, equal pay, and raising the minimum wage, since more than half of all workers earning that wage are women. One of her crowning achievements came in 2010, when she helped write President Obama's Affordable Care Act and secured the votes to pass it. Speaker Pelosi sees affordable health care, childcare, and housing as crucial to addressing her priority: "our children, our children, and our children." Her biggest motivator is that one out of every five children grows up in poverty.

She remembers having dinner at a friend's house as a child. After the meal, her friend's mother scraped the half-eaten food from everyone's plate into a bowl, so their family would have enough to eat the next day. Speaker Pelosi never forgot that.

"I grew up with a sense that public service was a noble calling," she told me. "It was all about making everything fairer for families."

Her father would literally offer constituents a seat at his dining room table. His belief in them helped them believe in themselves. Congresswoman Sala Burton's encouragement of Pelosi had the same effect, prompting her to consider claiming her own proverbial seat at the table.

In taking that seat, Speaker Pelosi led the way for a new generation of American women to take theirs.

A CONVERSATION WITH HOUSE SPEAKER NANCY PELOSI

(For a transcript of the complete interview, which took place on September 8, 2020, go to elisaboxer.com.)

Madam Speaker, how does someone who never intended to run for office become the highest-ranking woman in American politics?

Be ready, you never know what's around the next turn in your life! When Sala Burton came along, here was a *woman*, a member of Congress, making a decision about who she wanted to succeed her. That hardly ever happens. Men usually make the decisions.

So you checked with your daughter, who was going to be a senior in high school. . . .

Yes, I asked Alexandra. I said, "Any answer is okay. I love being home with you, and I'm happy to keep doing volunteer work." And she said, "Mother, get a life." What teenage girl wouldn't want her mom gone three nights a week? But she was very close to my husband, so I knew they'd get along great while I was in Washington.

How do you handle your critics?

I don't pay attention to them. You can't. You just have to know your "why" and know how you want to help improve people's lives.

What's your most important message for children reading this book?

Be yourself. Trust in who you are. Of course, it's nice to have mentors and people you admire. But authentically, you are you. Don't forget that. Know your power.

What does "knowing your power" mean to you, and how can young people apply it in their own lives?

If you have an opportunity, nobody can undertake it the way you can. Have confidence in that, and know the remarkable difference that only you can make when you have your seat at the table. There's no limit to what's possible.

I am very excited that in this Congress, on the hundredth anniversary of the Nineteenth Amendment, there are more than one hundred women in the House. It's a great thing for every little girl to look up and think there's no barrier for her.

SELECTED BIBLIOGRAPHY

For a list of websites and video sources, visit elisaboxer.com.

Articles

Associated Press. "Pelosi Wins Easily in S.F. Congress Race." *Los Angeles Times*, June 3, 1987.

Associated Press. "Speaker of the House Pelosi Makes History." NBCNews.com, January 3, 2007.

Campbell, Colin. "The D'Alesandros: A Baltimore Political Powerhouse That Gave Us Two Mayors and House Speaker Nancy Pelosi." *Baltimore Sun*, October 20, 2019.

Caygle, Heather, and Rachael Bade. "'Madame Speaker': Pelosi Reclaims the Gavel." *Politico*, January 3, 2019.

Epstein, Edward, and Zachary Coile. "Madam Speaker." *San Francisco Chronicle*, January 5, 2007.

Feuerherd, Joe. "Roots in Faith, Family and Party Guide Pelosi's Move to Power." *National Catholic Reporter*, January 24, 2003.

Hickey, Walt, Mariana Alfaro, and Grace Panetta. "Today Is Nancy Pelosi's 79th Birthday—Here's How She Went from San Francisco Housewife to the Most Powerful Woman in US Politics." *Business Insider*, March 26, 2019.

Killough, Ashley, and Beryl Adcock. "Pelosi Takes Speaker's Oath of Office Surrounded by Children." CNN Politics, January 3, 2019.

Lindsey, Robert. "House Race in West Goes to Runoff." *New York Times*, April 9, 1987.

McLaughlin, Kelly. "Nancy Pelosi Invited 'All Children' Up to the Podium as She Was Sworn in as House Speaker." *Business Insider*, January 3, 2019.

Stuart, Tessa, and Jann S. Wenner. "Nancy Pelosi: The Rolling Stone Interview." *Rolling Stone*, February 27, 2019.

Books

Bzdek, Vincent. *Woman of the House: The Rise of Nancy Pelosi.* New York: St. Martin's Press, 2008.

Leigh, Anna. *Nancy Pelosi: Political Powerhouse.* Gateway Biographies. Minneapolis: Lerner Publications, 2020.

Pelosi, Nancy, and Amy Hill Hearth. *Know Your Power: A Message to America's Daughters.* New York: Anchor, 2009.

Povich, Elaine. *Nancy Pelosi: A Biography.* Westport, CT: Greenwood, 2008.

Interview

Pelosi, Nancy, in discussion with the author via telephone, September 8, 2020.

Quotation Sources

8–9: "My father did the day job . . .": Nancy Pelosi, phone interview with author, September 8, 2020.

12–13: "encounter with history": Nancy Pelosi and Amy Hill Hearth, *Know Your Power: A Message to America's Daughters*, 28. "his electrifying call to public service": Nancy Pelosi, upon accepting the JFK Profile in Courage Award, May 20, 2019.

14–15: "Sometimes it takes . . .": Pelosi and Hearth, 7.

16–17: "I'm Nancy Pelosi, and I'm running for Congress": Pelosi and Hearth, 77.

18–19: "What is in your heart . . .": Pelosi and Hearth, 152.

20–21: *"At last, we have a seat at the table"*: Pelosi, interview.

22–23: "at the *head* of the table": @SpeakerPelosi Twitter post, December 10, 2019. "For our daughters . . .": Nancy Pelosi, acceptance speech upon receiving the gavel, January 4, 2007.

24–25: "I wanted to come back . . .": Matthew Hay Brown, "All Signs Point to Home," *Baltimore Sun*, January 6, 2007.

26–27: "When women succeed . . .": Marianne Schnall, "'Don't Agonize, Organize': Why Nancy Pelosi Wants More Women in Washington," Forbes.com, October 30, 2018.

30–31: "I am particularly proud . . .": John Parkinson, "Pelosi Repeats History, Recaptures the Speaker's Gavel," abcnews.go.com, January 3, 2019.

32–33: "message of strength": *60 Minutes Overtime*, "House Speaker Nancy Pelosi's Account of the Riot at the Capitol," cbsnews.com, January 10, 2021.

34–35: "old-boy politics": Pelosi and Hearth, 135. "anything is possible . . .": Associated Press, "Speaker of the House Pelosi Makes History," nbcnews.com, January 3, 2007. "our children . . .": Pelosi, interview. "I grew up . . .": Pelosi, interview.

For Daphne. May you grow up knowing your power.
And for Adrienne. Your voice is still heard.
—E.B.

To Mom, who encouraged and had faith in me . . .
and who always said exactly what was on her mind.
—L.F.